Seven Last Words

Seven
Last
Words

*An Invitation to a Deeper
Friendship with Jesus*

JAMES MARTIN, SJ

HarperOne
An Imprint of HarperCollinsPublishers

HarperOne

Portions of this book appeared, in a different form, in the author's
book *Jesus: A Pilgrimage*.

Imprimi Potest: Very Rev. John Cecero, SJ

HarperCollins books may be purchased for educational, business, or
sales promotional use. For information please e-mail the Special Mar-
kets Department at SPsales@harpercollins.com.

HarperCollins website: http://www.harpercollins.com

FIRST EDITION

Designed by Ralph Fowler

Library of Congress Cataloging-in-Publication Data
Martin, James, author.
  Seven last words : an invitation to a deeper friendship with Jesus /
James Martin, SJ.
     pages   cm
  ISBN 978-0-06-243138-7 (hardcover) — ISBN 978-0-06-243139-4
(e-book) — ISBN 978-0-06-244475-2 (audio)
  1. Jesus Christ—Seven last words. I. Title.
  BT457.M37   2015
  232.96'35—dc23   2015031519

16 17 18 19 20   RRD(H)   10 9 8 7 6 5 4 3 2 1

For all who have ever felt confused,
abandoned, or alone.

CONTENTS

At the time of this writing, St. Patrick's Cathedral is undergoing its first full-fledged restoration and renovation since its construction in 1858. As I sat in the cathedral on Good Friday in the midst of this physical renewal of our beloved cathedral, I listened to Father Martin's reflections on the Lord's Seven Last Words, grateful for the spiritual renewal he was bringing to the faithful assembled in prayer on this most solemn day of the church year.

I trust you will find these reflections as spiritually rewarding and uplifting as I.

—Timothy Michael Cardinal Dolan
Archbishop of New York
May 13, 2015
Year of Consecrated Life

The Seven
Last Words

When I mentioned to a friend that I had been invited to preach the "Seven Last Words" at St. Patrick's Cathedral in New York City, her reaction was not surprising: "The seven last *what*?"

Although prayer services centering on the Seven Last Words began, by some accounts, as early as the sixteenth century, many devout Christians are not familiar with the tradition. So a little background may be in order.

The Seven Last Words are the seven last sentences, or phrases, or sayings, uttered by Jesus as he hung on the cross on Good Friday, at least as recorded in the Gospels. (There may have been others that were not recorded.)

Traditionally, they are ordered as follows:

"Father, forgive them; for they do not know what they are doing." (Luke 23:34)

"Truly I tell you, today you will be with me in Paradise." (Luke 23:43)

"My God, my God, why have you forsaken me?" (Mark 15:34; Matthew 27:46)

"Woman, here is your son. . . . Here is your mother." (John 19:26–27)

"Father, into your hands I commend my spirit." (Luke 23:46)

"I am thirsty." (John 19:28)

"It is finished." (John 19:30)

A quick glance at that list shows that Jesus speaks one time in the Gospels of Matthew and Mark, three times in Luke, and three times in John. So the first question people often ask about the Seven Last Words is: Given the importance of these utterances, why doesn't each phrase appear in every Gospel? Indeed, if we treat Matthew and Mark as a unity (since Matthew probably drew upon Mark's Gospel), no saying in any of the Gospels appears in the others.[1] Why not?

To answer that, it's helpful to understand something about the New Testament. So let me offer a brief précis of the development of the Gospels.

The writing of the Gospels took place in several stages.[2] The first was Jesus's actual public ministry, which began roughly around 30 AD. Next came the "oral tradition," when stories of what Jesus said and did were passed along orally, from person to person. During this period, there would have been little need for a written record: Jesus's apostles, disciples, followers, and other eyewitnesses were around to offer firsthand accounts of their encounters with him. For some episodes there would have been many witnesses; for others, a small number; for a few, just one.[3] But there was no need for books when you had eyewitnesses. Besides, many of the early disciples could neither read nor write.

Even at this early stage, you can see the likelihood that differences would arise among the various oral traditions. To begin with, not all eyewitnesses would describe an event in precisely the same way. Each would stress one thing or another, depending on what each deemed important. Already we can see how variations could creep into the story of Jesus, which helps to answer the question of why the Gospels don't always agree with one another and, in this case, why all of the Seven Last Words aren't included in every Gospel.

After the original witnesses died (and it became clear that Jesus would not, as some expected, return soon), the next stage began. This required the editorial work of those who compiled the Gospels for the early church, known as the "evangelists": Matthew, Mark, Luke, and John.[4] Over time, the church settled on these four books as the approved, or "canonical," Gospels because of their widespread use, theological orthodoxy, and association with the apostles.[5]

Each evangelist wrote for a different audience and so stressed different parts of the story, perhaps leaving out what another writer would deem important or adding passages that another writer would consider less significant. This also helps to explain the selection of some of Jesus's sayings from the cross and the omission of others. Moreover, some of the sayings of Jesus from the cross may have been known to one evangelist, but perhaps not to the others.

Three of the Gospels—Matthew, Mark and Luke—are intertwined. Although there are competing theories about *how* they are connected, it is clear that they are. Most scholars think that Mark's Gospel came first and that the evangelist wrote to a non-Jewish community around 70 AD. Matthew's Gospel, written around 85 or 90 and addressed to a primarily Jewish audience, is an expanded and revised version of Mark, supplemented with other stories. Luke, though likely a Gentile (or non-Jew), nonetheless knew something about Jewish traditions when he wrote his Gospel around the same time as Matthew; he also drew on Mark and supplemented his narrative with other stories. Both Matthew and Luke also relied heavily on an independent source of sayings.[6]

Although Matthew, Mark, and Luke edited their books to address specific communities of readers, their Gospels are so similar that they are referred to as the Synoptic Gospels, because they include numerous passages that can be looked at together. (The Greek *syn-opsis* means, roughly, "see together.")

The Gospel of John, written later, most likely for Christians in the eastern Mediterranean area in the late first century, is noticeably different from the Synoptics. John's narrative, for example, introduces several characters who do not appear at all in the other three Gospels, including

Nicodemus, the man born blind, the Samaritan woman, and Lazarus. In fact, few of the episodes of Jesus's public ministry recorded in John mirror those in the Synoptics.

Thus, it's easy to see why the Seven Last Words might vary from Gospel to Gospel. These phrases, then, represent not only Jesus's final thoughts on the cross (at least as recorded in the Gospels), but also what the original communities for which the evangelists wrote considered to be the most important sayings. So the Seven Last Words are important for understanding not only Jesus, but also the early church.

Now that we know a little about the Gospels, where did the tradition of worship services centered on the Seven Last Words arise?

That's harder to explain. As early as the second century, there were attempts to "order" the Seven Last Words to give them some coherence.[7] Some scholars, as I mentioned, date liturgical ceremonies that center on the sayings as far back as the sixteenth century, but it is difficult to pinpoint their origins with precision.

Today, at the very least, we can say that the current practice extends throughout churches in various Christian denominations and is usually a part of the Good Friday service in a cathedral or church. Composers have also used the Seven Last Words as settings for chorale pieces. Normally, the liturgies of the Seven Last Words include some combination of prayer, music, and reflections.

Most churches choose seven different speakers, sometimes from various Christian denominations, each of whom reflects on one of the sayings. In the Jesuit church in New York where I often celebrate Mass, the pastor usually invites Episcopal priests (both men and women), Baptist pastors, Lutheran clergy, members of Catholic religious orders, and laypeople from various walks of life for a wide variety of perspectives on Good Friday. In my case, Cardinal Timothy Dolan, the archbishop of New York, asked me to be the sole presenter, which prompted more than a few Jesuits to exclaim, with no little concern for the parishioners at St. Patrick's, "All seven? Just *you*?"

If there is an overarching theme in my own reflections, it is the way that Jesus's sufferings help him to understand us. Few insights have been as important in my own life and in the lives of people who come to me for spiritual direction and pastoral counseling. The person to whom we pray, the man we hope to follow, the one who is risen from the dead, *understands* us—because he lived a human life, and one that, particularly in his final week, was filled with suffering.

Of course, this is hardly a new insight. The Letter to the Hebrews says, "For we do not have a high priest who is unable to sympathize with our weaknesses, but we have one who in every respect has been tested as we are, yet without sin."[8]

This is not to say that suffering is the only important part of Jesus's life. Indeed, there has been throughout Christian history an over-emphasis on the sufferings of Jesus. To focus on him purely as the "Man of Sorrows" overlooks the rest of his public ministry, which was one of great joy.

Can there be any doubt that Jesus was a joyful person who brought joy to others? Jesus's healings—of a man who had been paralyzed for thirty-eight years, of a woman who had been sick for twelve years, of a little girl who was thought to be dead, to take but a few examples— were the source not only of amazement, but joy. And according to many New Testament scholars, many of his lighthearted parables and sayings would have been seen not simply as wise and clever, but laugh-out-loud funny.[9]

Indeed, some of the people at the time accused Jesus of being *too* lighthearted, and he admits as much when he compares his reception with John the Baptist's: "For John came neither eating nor drinking, and they say, 'He has a demon'; the Son of Man came eating and drinking, and they say, 'Look, a glutton and a drunkard, a friend of tax collectors and sinners!' "[10]

In other words, Jesus says that he is being critiqued for, as one biblical scholar put it to me, "living it up." He was seen, at least by some, as not "serious" enough. His first miracle, after all, was to make more wine at a party. Jesus, we need to remember, was a fully human person; as such, he had a fully human sense of humor and even of fun. The Man of Sorrows was, more often, the Man of Joys.

Nonetheless, this book focuses mainly on how his sufferings on Good Friday enable him to understand us. Of course, Jesus is fully human and fully divine, and so he participates in divine knowledge. But because he was fully human, to paraphrase Hebrews, we do not relate to a God who is removed from our experiences. We do not pray to a God who does not appreciate the difficulties of our lives. We do not have a God who looks down on us from on high and merely pities us, as a wealthy person might pass a homeless person on the street and say, "What a shame."

Rather, we have a God who suffered intensely and, as we will see, suffered many of the same things that we suffer. Thus we have a compassionate God, a sympathetic God, an empathetic God, a God who understands our lives because he *experienced* our lives. It is the deepest form of understanding and compassion the world has ever seen. And in these brief meditations I would like to invite you to come to know, and enter into a deeper relationship with, this God who understands us.

I

Jesus Understands the Challenge of Forgiveness

"Father, forgive them; for they do not know what they are doing."

As they led him away, they seized a man, Simon of Cyrene, who was coming from the country, and they laid the cross on him, and made him carry it behind Jesus. A great number of the people followed him, and among them were women who were beating their breasts and wailing for him. But Jesus turned to them and said, "Daughters of Jerusalem, do not weep for me, but weep for yourselves and for your children. For the days are surely coming when they will say, 'Blessed are the barren, and the wombs that never bore, and the breasts that never nursed.' Then they will begin to say to the mountains, 'Fall on us'; and to the hills, 'Cover us.' For if they do this when the wood is green, what will happen when it is dry?"

Two others also, who were criminals, were led away to be put to death with him. When they came to the place that is called The Skull, they crucified Jesus there with the criminals, one on his right and one on his left. Then Jesus said, "Father, forgive them; for they do not know what they are doing." And they cast lots to divide his clothing. And the people stood by, watching; but the leaders scoffed at him, saying, "He saved others; let him save himself if he is the Messiah of God, his chosen one!" The soldiers also mocked him, coming up and offering him sour wine and saying, "If you are the King of the Jews, save yourself!"

I n our sometimes dark world we are often given moments of light that not only illu- mine our way, but remind us that God is with us.

One kind of these moments happens fre- quently, and you've probably heard about it, read about it, or even encountered it yourself. I'm speaking about moments of radical forgive- ness: those amazing stories, which you've seen in newspapers, on television, or online, of men and women forgiving people responsible for horrific crimes committed against them or, more typi- cally, against members of their families.

A Jesuit friend, for example, once told me a moving story about his family. One night, his father was awakened from a deep sleep and told that his sixteen-year-old son had been killed in a car accident while being driven by a friend named Kenny, who was drunk at the time. At the trial, the father pleaded with the judge to give Kenny the minimum sentence possible, because Kenny never wanted to kill his friend.

Afterward, my Jesuit friend asked his father how he could possibly do that. His father said, "I just did what I thought was right." He also said that he saw Kenny as more than just that one terrible act. Today, my friend's father still keeps in touch with Kenny, who now has his own children. For his part, Kenny has written faithfully for the last twenty years to the father of the boy whose death he caused.

And recently *America* magazine, where I work as an editor, published the remarkable story of a woman named Jeanne—an attorney, as it happens—who forgave the man who killed her sister, her sister's husband, and their unborn child.[1] The killer was remorseless and had never admitted his guilt.

Now here is a story of not an accidental death, but an intentional one, and—let me repeat—there was no remorse. I repeat that because many people believe you can't forgive someone who isn't sorry.

But Jeanne *was* able to forgive her sister's murderer. She said that at the time the phrase "You take away the sins of the world," which Catholics recite during the Mass, deeply moved her. Jeanne said she wasn't sure if she'd ever fully understand what those words mean, but they surely don't mean that we should take the sin a person commits and freeze it; that no matter what the person does, even if he or she repents, we should punish the person for it forever. It's similar to what Sister Helen Prejean, CSJ, the author of *Dead Man Walking,* often says about inmates on death row: "People are more than the worst thing they've ever done in their lives."

Years later, Jeanne realized that she had never told her sister's murderer that she had forgiven him. So she wrote him a letter and did so.

In response, Jeanne received a letter of confession and remorse. He wrote, "You're right, I am guilty of killing your sister . . . and her husband. . . . I also want to take this opportunity to express my deepest condolences and apologize to you."

Forgiveness had freed him to be honest and remorseful.

I'm sure you've heard stories like this. I'm sure you've also seen occasions of the more common situation, where victims are given the opportunity in the courtroom to respond to the criminals, and they do *not* forgive. I'm sure you've seen videos of family members screaming at criminals: "I want you to suffer like I am!" "I hope you rot in jail!" "I hope you fry in the electric chair!" "I hope you go to hell!" It's understandable. Anyone who is the victim of a crime or the relative or friend of a victim—particularly of a violent crime—should be forgiven for being angry. I would probably feel the same way. It's human.

But the reason we respond so powerfully to those other situations, where radical forgiveness is offered, is that they're *divine*. That's why they touch us. Those moments speak to the deepest part of ourselves, which instinctively recognizes the divine. We see these moments as beautiful, because this is how God wants us to live. It's a kind of call.

Now you may say, "Those are nice words, Father, but you don't live in the real world. What do you know about that?"

Let me assure you, even in religious orders and in the priesthood one can find anger, bitterness, and ill will. But it's easy to see where people get that idea. I'm sometimes susceptible to that kind of romanticism myself. Once I said to a Benedictine monk, "Well, I'm sure it's easier in a monastery than it is in a Jesuit community."

He just laughed and told me a funny story. One elderly monk in his community used to show his displeasure with other monks in a highly creative way. As you may know, most monastic communities chant the psalms several times a day together in chapel. Well, if this elderly monk was angry at someone, every time the word "enemy" came up in a psalm, as in "Deliver me from my enemies," he would look up from his prayer book and glare at the monk he was angry with.[2]

On a more personal note, I once lived in a community with a Jesuit who more or less refused to talk to me for ten years. He despised me and made that clear in almost every interaction we had—whether alone or in a group. At one point, I asked him if I had done anything to offend him, and he refused to answer. I never figured out what prompted his hatred, and he never changed his attitude. In desperation, I asked an elderly Jesuit priest, renowned for his holiness, for advice.

The only thing to do, he told me, is to forgive.

The only thing to do is forgive. Because it's the only thing that can free both parties. It frees one person from the prison of resentment and from seeing the other as less than human. And it frees the other person in some way. As the father of my Jesuit friend discovered. As Kenny, the drunk driver, discovered. As Jeanne, the attorney, discovered. And as her sister's murderer discovered. We may not know *how* it will free the other person, and it may be in a way that we will never see, but it will.

Now, you might be thinking of a situation in your own life and say, "I can never forgive. It's impossible." Maybe a spouse has cheated on you, or a friend has betrayed you, or a business partner has defrauded you. You may say, "The sin is too great." Well, think about those two stories of forgiveness you just read.

Then look at what Jesus does from the cross. If anyone had the right *not* to forgive, it was Jesus. If anyone had the right to lash out in anger, it was Jesus. If anyone had the right to feel unjustly persecuted, it was Jesus. Yet even though the Roman soldiers do not express remorse in front of him, Jesus not only forgives them; he prays for them. Notice that. Jesus says, "Father, forgive them." He's praying for them.

Now consider that line, "They do not know what they are doing." That's a helpful insight. In the case of Jesus on the cross, most scholars believe that that phrase probably means, "They don't know that they are doing this to God's Son."[3] But that particular phrase helped me a great deal with the Jesuit who wouldn't speak to me. He didn't seem to know what he was doing. Indeed, people who sin sometimes don't seem to be thinking clearly. This insight may help you on your road to forgiveness. It's the same impulse that allows you to easily forgive a mentally ill person for doing something that seems thoughtless, rude, or even cruel.

Both my friend's father and Jeanne saw the people who had sinned against them not simply as that single act, but as human beings. Jesus does the same thing.

Jesus always *sees*. And he sees beyond what people around him see. He sees people for who they really are. When he first meets Peter, for example, he doesn't see just a poor fisherman from a small town beside the Sea of Galilee;

he sees someone with the potential to lead a church.[4] When he meets Zacchaeus, the chief tax collector in Jericho, he doesn't see just the most sinful person in the region—for that's how the chief tax collector would have been seen by his fellow Jews—he sees someone seeking redemption.[5] When he sees the woman caught in adultery, he doesn't see just her sin; he sees a person in need of forgiveness and healing.[6]

Jesus does the same from the cross. He doesn't see just executioners. He sees people making horrible decisions and perhaps being forced to do so. He sees them, and so he loves them, and so he can forgive them. Forgiveness is a gift you give the other person and yourself. Jesus knows this. And he not only tells us this several times in the Gospels, but he *shows* us this. He is teaching us even from the cross.

Now, here's the big question: How do you do it? You may want to forgive but feel incapable of doing so. You want to let go of resentment, but you may honestly feel that you don't have that power within you.

Well, that *wanting* is a good start, because true forgiveness is a gift from God. It's a grace. Moreover, to paraphrase St. Ignatius Loyola, the founder of the Jesuit Order, even if you don't have the desire to forgive, if you have the *desire for the desire,* that's enough. God can work with that.

So you may think, "Well, I can't do it."

And you're right.

You can't.

But God can.

2

Jesus Understands Doubts About the Afterlife

"Truly I tell you, today you will be with me in Paradise."

One of the criminals who were hanged there kept deriding him and saying, "Are you not the Messiah? Save yourself and us!" But the other rebuked him, saying, "Do you not fear God, since you are under the same sentence of condemnation? And we indeed have been condemned justly, for we are getting what we deserve for our deeds, but this man has done nothing wrong." Then he said, "Jesus, remember me when you come into your kingdom." He replied, "Truly I tell you, today you will be with me in Paradise."

Believing in the afterlife is a significant problem for many people, even for some devout believers. And without a belief in the afterlife, fear of the unknown often takes over. It's one of the most common fears in the whole Christian life.

You might be surprised to learn, for example, that St. Thérèse of Lisieux, the French Carmelite nun known as the "Little Flower" and one of the most well-known saints, struggled with this very fear as she confronted death. Though Thérèse trusted in God for her entire life, when she faced her final illness, she suffered serious doubts about the afterlife. "If you only knew what darkness I am plunged into," she said to one of the sisters in her Carmelite community.

"I don't believe in eternal life; I think that after this life there is nothing."[1]

It's not hard to wonder about this. None of us are completely free of doubt in the spiritual life. And in those moments of doubt, we may ask ourselves: What awaits me after I die? Is all of this faith in vain? Will I really be rewarded for the good deeds I did while on earth? Or punished for the bad things I did? What has happened to the people I loved? Will I ever see them again?

Without breaking any confidences, I can say that even many devout believers who come to me for spiritual direction have a hard time with this.

But here, in this saying from the cross, Jesus promises the hope of the afterlife, of "paradise," to the person traditionally called the "Good Thief."

This is not the first time that Jesus speaks about the afterlife. It's one of several places in the Gospels where Jesus holds out that promise. In the Gospel of John, immediately before

Jesus raises Lazarus from the dead, he says to Martha, the dead man's sister, "Those who believe in me, even though they die, will live, and everyone who lives and believes in me will never die."[2] Later in John's Gospel, at the Last Supper, as Jesus is preparing to take leave of his disciples, he says, "In my Father's house there are many dwelling places. . . . I go to prepare a place for you."[3]

Jesus, who heard the doubts of people in his lifetime, understands doubt—even doubts about the afterlife. So the first thing that should convince us of the promise of the afterlife is this: Jesus tells us. And, needless to say, Jesus is not a liar.

This utterance from the cross, incidentally, is the only time that Jesus uses the word "paradise" in all of the Gospels. He is responding to the Good Thief, who, you'll notice, calls him "Jesus." That's a very familiar way of speaking to him. The disciples, on the other hand, almost always call him "Teacher," "Master," or

"Rabbi." Usually only the demons and those seeking healing use the name "Jesus," which in Hebrew means "the Lord saves."

It's beautiful to recall that this was the name given to him at the Annunciation, when the Angel Gabriel told Mary what to call her son. It's the name that Mary and Joseph called him when he was a baby: "Don't cry, Jesus," they may have said, "it's okay." It's the name his extended family used when he was growing up in Nazareth: "Joseph," they would ask, "how is your son Jesus doing?" It's the name his friends used when they called to him to play games: "Jesus! Jesus! Over here!" It's the name that the adults in Nazareth used every day: "That Jesus is a good carpenter."

But in his public ministry that name wasn't used as frequently by his disciples or even friends like Martha and Mary, who also called him "Teacher," "Rabbi," or "Master." Maybe he hadn't heard the name very much lately. Maybe he missed being called by the name his parents used. But now, on the cross, his name is used by a stranger, a repentant sinner, someone who asks him for help one last time.

The Good Thief shows us who the one next to him is. A man, yes. A man with a simple name, Jesus. But God too. The man who can open paradise for him.

And Jesus responds. At the hour of his human death, the divine one reveals what God has in store for us. From the cross, Jesus tells the Good Thief, and us, about the future that is planned for us. Even in his agony, he offers the man a kind of spiritual healing. So one of Jesus's last acts before his earthly death is a healing. "Don't worry," he's saying. "There is a heaven."

So we need to take Jesus at his word.

Then on Easter Sunday Jesus does something even greater. He doesn't simply tell us about eternal life; he *shows* us. Modern writers often say, "Show. Don't tell." That is, tell the story simply rather than overexplaining. St. Ignatius Loyola often said, "Love shows itself more readily in deeds than in words." Or as we would say today, "Actions speak louder than words." On Easter Sunday, at the Resurrection, Jesus *shows us* the future God has in store for us.

St. Paul, in his First Letter to the Corinthians, says that Jesus is the "first fruits of those who have died."[4] What does that mean? Well, in those days, the "first fruits" were the first grains, fruits, or other crops that were harvested, which were then offered to God as a thanksgiving for God's faithfulness.

The Hebrew people were supposed to offer God, for example, a sheaf of the first grain harvested on the day after the Sabbath following the Passover feast.[5] Then came the rest of the harvest. Paul is using the term "first fruits" to underline the certainty of the resurrection. First comes Christ, who is raised from the dead, never to die; then come all those who believe in him. We will follow him in the harvest.

When people in first-century Palestine encountered Jesus, they encountered the reign of God, what God has planned for us. When the sick encountered him, they were healed of their illnesses. When the deaf encountered him, they were able to hear. When the lame encountered him, they were able to walk. When the poor encountered him, the good news was preached to them. When those on the margins encountered him, they were restored to community. When sinners encountered him, they were forgiven.

Encountering Jesus means encountering the reign of God. And after his Resurrection, encountering Jesus means encountering the fullness of what God has in store for us: eternal life.

So we have Jesus's word telling us about the afterlife and we have the Resurrection showing us this. But let me share another way that helps those struggling with questions about the afterlife.

Let's begin with a fundamental truth: God is in a loving relationship with you. At the moment of your conception, God invited you into a relationship, and that has been manifesting itself in many ways ever since. That relationship manifests itself in peak moments, when God feels so close you could almost touch God: for instance, when you look at the face of your newborn child and can't believe how much love you feel welling up inside you, when you see a sunrise and are overwhelmed by the beauty of creation, or when you hear a familiar hymn that moves you to tears. That relationship also reveals itself in more common daily moments that make you aware of God's presence: when someone offers you a kind word in the midst of a painful time, when you feel the first warm springtime breeze after a seemingly endless winter, when you hear a line from the Gospels that hits your heart like an arrow.

As you look back over your life and ponder these moments, you can see the presence of God. These are signs of God's being in a loving relationship with you.

Here's my point: why would God ever destroy the loving relationship God has with you? That makes no sense. Could something as small as death destroy that relationship?

By no means! As St. Paul says in the Letter to the Romans, not even death can separate us from the love of God.[6] That relationship will last, as will our relationships with those who have gone before us. How could God possibly destroy that love? Our friends and family who have died will one day be reunited with us—in the place that God has prepared for us. God would never destroy love and so would never destroy the loving relationships God has with us or the ones we have with one another.

One day, we pray, we will be with Jesus in paradise. We have Jesus's word on it. We have Easter as proof. And we know that God would never destroy the loving relationships God has with us.

And one day, like the Good Thief, we will see that it is all true.

~ **3** ~

Jesus Understands a Parent's Love

"Woman, here is your son. . . .
Here is your mother."

When Jesus saw his mother and the disciple whom he loved standing beside her, he said to his mother, "Woman, here is your son." Then he said to the disciple, "Here is your mother." And from that hour the disciple took her into his own home.

It's a safe bet to say that most Catholics and many readers of this book have prayed the Rosary. At the very least, many Catholics have said a Hail Mary at least once or twice in their lives and asked for prayers from the Mother of God. In short, it's a fair bet to say that many Catholics have a devotion to the Blessed Mother.

Whenever I hear the phrase "the Blessed Mother," I think of my Aunt Rose, who was also my godmother. My family is from Philadelphia, and that's where my Aunt Rose and Uncle Larry spent their entire lives, in a small row house, where they raised their three children. Whenever Aunt Rose wanted good weather, she would put a statue of the Blessed Mother in her window, facing outward.

On her daughter's wedding day, Aunt Rose placed the statue of the Blessed Mother on a windowsill. Happily, and perhaps thanks to Mary's prayers, it turned out to be a beautiful day.

But if, for some reason, my aunt placed the statue in the window and the weather was in any way inclement, Mary would be removed from the windowsill and placed on a bookshelf, with her back turned toward us. When she told me that, I asked, "Are you scolding Mary?" And we laughed at that.

The most moving story about my aunt's devotion came when her husband had a heart attack and was on the verge of death. Frightened, the two of them sat on their bed and recited the Rosary until the ambulance came. A few hours later he died. When I was preparing the homily for his funeral Mass, it struck me that the phrase from the Hail Mary "now and at the hour of our death," which the two of them had prayed all their lives, was never more real for them.[1]

So, many of us, like my aunt and uncle, are devoted to the Blessed Mother.

But let's look at Mary in another way. And I'd like to invite you to use a model that we often use for Jesus.

Christians believe that Jesus Christ is fully human and fully divine. Now, some Christians relate more to the *human* Jesus, the man who walked the landscape of first-century Palestine, who has a body, who feels what we feel, and who is really and truly one of us.[2] Other Christians relate more to the *divine* Jesus, the one who has been raised from the dead, who reigns in heaven. Put another way, some people relate more to Jesus of Nazareth, others to Our Lord Jesus Christ. That's both natural and okay—as long as we remember they're the same person, that Jesus is always both fully human and fully divine.

Something similar is true about Mary. Now, Mary is a fully human person, not divine like Jesus. But still, people relate to her in two main ways. Many of us, like my aunt and uncle, relate more to the Blessed Mother, the Queen of Heaven, the Mother of God, the one who is praying for us in heaven.

But I'd like to invite you to think about Mary in another way. I'd like to invite you to think about Miriam of Nazareth, a woman living in a backwater village in Galilee.

Mary, as you probably know, was chosen by God while she was a young girl to bear Jesus. Mary was perhaps fourteen or fifteen years old when she had her mysterious encounter with the Angel Gabriel.

Many Christians idealize Mary. We think, *How wonderful it must have been to have been chosen for this! How marvelous to have been the mother of Jesus! What a grace-filled life she led!*

Although Mary did indeed lead a grace-filled life, we cannot forget that this real-life woman almost certainly experienced a great deal of confusion. That confusion began at the Annunciation. When told that she would conceive and bear a son, she asked the angel, "How can this be, since I am a virgin?"[3] Notice, then, that Mary's very first utterance in the Gospels is an expression of confusion.

There is more confusion in store for her after Jesus starts his public ministry. Of course she had the benefit of the Angel Gabriel's original message, but still we can ask: Between the Annunciation and her first witnessing of Jesus's miracles, did Mary have a spiritual experience that was equally profound? Or did she have to rely on what was revealed to her at the Annunciation?

Why do I ask this? Because at one point in the Gospels, Mary is obviously disturbed by her son's actions. Soon after Jesus begins his public ministry, Mary travels with the rest of Jesus's extended family from Nazareth to Capernaum, a distance of roughly forty miles, to collect him. After they arrive in Capernaum, Jesus is told, "Your mother and your brothers and sisters are outside, asking for you."[4] Apparently, they had come to bring him back to Nazareth. One Gospel verse says that Mary and the family have come to "restrain" him![5]

In response, Jesus looks to his followers who are gathered around him, and says, "Who are my mother and my brothers?" Then, pointing to his disciples, he says, "Here are my mother and my brothers! Whoever does the will of God is my brother and sister and mother."[6]

There are many ways to read this passage—and perhaps Jesus did eventually greet his mother and his family in Capernaum. But on the face of it, Jesus is reminding his listeners that familial ties are not as important as ties between the teacher and his disciples. It must have been a difficult thing for his mother to hear. In his commentary on the Gospel of Matthew, the New Testament scholar Daniel J. Harrington, SJ, notes, "As in Mark, it expresses an alienation, or even separation, on Jesus's part from his own family."[7]

So Jesus's ministry might have been confusing for Mary. And it was surely painful, as it would be for any mother, to watch him leave home. And by this point Joseph, Mary's husband, would have been dead. How do we know? One clear indication is that when Jesus's family goes to collect him in Capernaum, Joseph is not with them.[8] Also, Joseph is not present at the Crucifixion. So we can presume that he has died. We can also presume that Jesus mourned Joseph and keenly felt his absence as he carried out his public ministry.

But even if he needed to distance himself as he began his public ministry, Jesus loved his family. Interestingly, one reason that Jesus may have waited to begin his ministry until roughly the age of thirty, which was a late age to begin a "career" (life expectancies in Nazareth were between thirty and forty years at the time), was to ensure that Mary was provided for. Significantly, Mary does not remarry, as she could have. Therefore, it's reasonable to conclude that someone provided her with enough money to live on after her husband's death. Who? Most likely Jesus.

Recently I heard the story of a politician who waited for many years before he sought political office. He wanted to ensure that his daughter, who had developmental problems, was cared for. Something similar may have happened in Jesus's life.

Eventually, Mary comes to understand her son's ministry. In fact, at the Wedding Feast at Cana, it is she who prompts Jesus to perform what is traditionally considered his first miracle.[9] She informs Jesus that the party's hosts have run out of wine. "Woman," he says to her, "what concern is that to you and to me?" (Addressing your mother as "woman" was as sharp a comment in those days as it would be today.)

In response, Mary tells the stewards, "Do whatever he tells you." Jesus then asks the stewards to fill the large jars with water. They do. But when they draw out the liquid, it's not water that they discover, but wine.

The sequence of these two incidents may not be precise: it's difficult to determine the timing of the Wedding Feast at Cana and Jesus's family coming to "restrain" him in Capernaum, since the stories appear in two different Gospels. Nonetheless, it's likely that Mary went through her own journey of understanding Jesus. She moves from confusion about his ministry, which prompts her to come to Capernaum, to encouraging him to begin his miracle working in Cana. Eventually, Mary surmounts her confusion or at least begins to understand how to respond to her son. Indeed, she seems to grasp Jesus's vocation before he does—perhaps because she's had more time to think about it.

Imagine yourself now with Miriam of Nazareth. She's had a strange life. Chosen by God to do something that confused her at first. Asked to raise a son who, though we know little about his early life, was surely a unique child. Now imagine that son in Nazareth announcing that he's leaving to preach the good news. Imagine Mary disturbed by what he's doing. Next, imagine her coming to a greater understanding of his vocation and encouraging him to be who he was called to be. Then imagine her amazed at his power. And finally, in awe of who her son is.

Now imagine Mary, after that complicated life, standing at the foot of the cross. Imagine what it would have been like to hear her son say to her, "Woman, here is your son," and to the Beloved Disciple, "Here is your mother."

What is Jesus doing in his last moments? He's caring for Mary. Even helpless on the cross he is caring for her. Jesus understood both the love of a parent and love for a parent.

A question: Before this moment in Jesus's life, before his time on the cross, when was he the most helpless and vulnerable? When he was an infant. Moreover, God chose to come among us in the most helpless form imaginable—a child, utterly dependent on others. God was dependent on us. And who cared most for God in his helplessness? Mary. Now, helpless again, he helps her.

We don't have to be strong to help other people. We don't have to have money. We don't have to have professional training. We don't have to have academic degrees. We don't even have to be healthy. We only have to love and want to help.

In our helplessness we can always help. At the beginning of his life, Mary helped the helpless infant Jesus. At the end of his life, the helpless Jesus helped Mary.

When you ask for the prayers of the Blessed Mother, then, you are not only praying to the Queen of Heaven, the Mother of God, but also to Miriam of Nazareth, a woman who had a difficult life, who knows confusion, who knows heartache, who knows what it means to be loved and helped by Jesus. And who knows you.

Now and at the hour of your death.

4

Jesus Understands Feelings of Abandonment

"My God, my God, why have you forsaken me?"

When it was noon, darkness came over the whole land until three in the afternoon. At three o'clock Jesus cried out with a loud voice, "Eloi, Eloi, lema sabachthani?" which means, "My God, my God, why have you forsaken me?" When some of the bystanders heard it, they said, "Listen, he is calling for Elijah." And someone ran, filled a sponge with sour wine, put it on a stick, and gave it to him to drink, saying, "Wait, let us see whether Elijah will come to take him down." Then Jesus gave a loud cry and breathed his last. And the curtain of the temple was torn in two, from top to bottom. Now when the centurion, who stood facing him, saw that in this way he breathed his last, he said, "Truly this man was God's Son!"

"**E**loi, Eloi, lema sabachthani?" What are we to make of these extraordinary words? For some Christians, they are almost unbearable. Can it be true that Jesus thought that God the Father had forsaken him? Is it possible that Jesus doubted the love of the one he called *Abba,* "Father"? Did Jesus give up hope when he was crucified? Did he despair when he was on the cross?

There are two main ways of understanding these mysterious words of Jesus, which he quotes from Psalm 22 and which would have been recognizable to any Jewish person at the time who had received religious training.

The first possibility is that Jesus's words are not an expression of abandonment but, paradoxically, an expression of hope in God. Although Psalm 22 begins "My God, my God, why have you forsaken me?" and expresses the frustration of someone who feels abandoned by God, the second part of the psalm is a hymn of thanksgiving to God, who has heard the psalmist's prayer:

> *For he did not despise or abhor*
>   *the affliction of the afflicted;*
> *he did not hide his face from me,*
>   *but heard when I cried to him.*[1]

In this interpretation, Jesus is invoking the psalm in its *totality* as the prayer of one who cried out to God and was heard. An example based on a more well known psalm might be someone who says, "The Lord is my shepherd," and trusts that hearers would be familiar with the rest of Psalm 23 ("Even though I walk through the darkest valley . . .") and its overall message. In other words, saying, "The Lord is my shepherd" is usually taken not just as an affirmation of God as shepherd, but as shorthand for the entire psalm. This is a frequent explanation of Jesus's terrible cry from the cross. In short, Jesus was using that line from Psalm 22 to express his confidence in God.

But there is another possibility: Jesus really *did* feel abandoned. This is not to say that Jesus despaired. I don't believe that someone who had such an intimate relationship with the Father, with *Abba,* could have lost all *belief* in the presence of the Father in this dark moment. But it is not unreasonable to imagine Jesus, in this grave hour, *feeling* as if the Father were absent. And remember, if he's crying out to God, he's still in relationship with God.

Here we need to distinguish between a person's *believing* that God is absent and *feeling* it. The latter is common in the spiritual life. You may have had this experience yourself: believing in God, but not feeling that God is close. You ask, basically, "Where are you, God?" Here is another important intersection between Jesus's life and our own.

Of all people, Jesus could be forgiven for feeling abandoned. Think of what he has gone through by this point in the Passion. First, he's witnessed his betrayal by Judas, one of his closest friends, who had identified him to the authorities in exchange for thirty pieces of silver. Today we tend to think of Judas as purely evil, *always* evil, but remember that Jesus had selected him as one of the twelve apostles, and so for a time Jesus must have been close to Judas. Judas was a friend who betrayed him. Also, the Gospel of Mark says that by this point all but one of the apostles have fled, whether out of terror, confusion, or shame. So Jesus almost certainly feels abandoned and experiences, perhaps not for the first time in his life, human loneliness.

Jesus has also been subjected to an exhausting series of late-night inquests, brutalized by Roman guards, and marched through the streets of Jerusalem under a crushing weight; he is now nailed to the wood and suffering excruciating pain. So he could be forgiven for feeling abandoned. The one who abandoned himself to the

Father's will in the garden of Gethsemane the night before, who had given himself entirely to what the Father had in store for him, now wonders on the cross: "Where are you?"

These feelings were probably intensified by his having been abandoned by his followers. Until this point, if Jesus felt lonely or misunderstood by the disciples, he might have turned to the Father for comfort. Now he goes there and feels alone. It may be the loneliest any human being has ever felt.

Let me now turn to some biblical scholarship. One of the great twentieth-century New Testament scholars, Raymond E. Brown, a Sulpician priest, is the author of probably the definitive study of the Passion narratives, called *The Death of the Messiah*. In an essay entitled "Jesus's Death Cry," Father Brown says that, in his view, abandonment was in fact what Jesus was experiencing.[2]

Some Christians, says Father Brown, might want to reject the literal interpretation that would imply feelings of abandonment: "They could not attribute to Jesus such anguish in the face of death." Yet, as Brown says, if we accept that Jesus in the garden could still call the Father *Abba,* then we should accept this "screamed protest against abandonment wrenched from an utterly forlorn Jesus who now is so isolated and estranged that he no longer uses 'Father' language but speaks as the humblest servant."

What does Father Brown mean? When Jesus speaks to the Father in the garden, he says, "Abba, Father, for you all things are possible; remove this cup from me . . ."[3] *Abba* is a familiar way of speaking, something like saying "Dad." (Both times I have visited Jerusalem on pilgrimage, I have seen, in the crowded city streets, young children running to catch up with their fathers shouting, *"Abba! Abba!"*)

But on the cross, when Jesus says, "My God, my God," he uses the Aramaic word *Eloi* (or the Hebrew *Eli,* depending on the Gospel). That's a more formal way of speaking to God. The shift from the familiar *Abba* in the garden to the more formal *Eloi* on the cross is heartbreaking. Jesus's feeling of distance, then, reveals itself not only in the scream and not only in the line of the psalm that he utters, but also in the word *Eloi*.

How could Jesus feel abandoned? How could someone who had enjoyed an intimate relationship with the Father express such an emotion? To answer that, it may help to consider a similar situation closer to our own time.

In her early years, Blessed Teresa of Calcutta, the foundress of the Missionaries of Charity, enjoyed several mystical experiences of intense closeness with God. She also experienced that rarest of spiritual graces—a locution: she actually heard God's voice. And then—nothing. For the last fifty or so years of her life, until her death, she felt a sense of great emptiness in her prayer. At one point, she wrote to her confessor, "In my soul I feel just that terrible pain of loss—of God not wanting me—of God not being God—of God not really existing."[4]

When her journals and letters were published not long after her death, some readers were shocked by these sentiments, finding it difficult to understand how she could continue as a believer and indeed flourish as a religious leader. But Mother Teresa was expressing some very human feelings of abandonment and speaking of what spiritual writers call the "dark night." This state of being moves close to, but does not accept, despair.

In time, Mother Teresa's questions about God's existence faded, and she began to see this searing experience as an invitation to unite herself more closely with Jesus in his abandonment on the cross and with the poor, who also feel abandoned. Mother Teresa's letters do not mean that she had abandoned God or that God had abandoned her. In fact, in continuing with her ministry to the poor, she made a radical act of fidelity based on a relationship she still believed in—even if she could not sense God's presence. She trusted that earlier experience.

In other words, she had faith.

Jesus does not despair. He is still in relationship with *Abba*—calling on him from the cross. In the midst of horrific physical pain, abandoned by all but a few of his friends, and facing his imminent death, when it would be almost impossible for anyone to think lucidly, he might have felt abandoned. To me this makes more sense than the proposition that the psalm he quoted was meant to refer to God's salvation.

So Jesus understands not only our bodily suffering, but also our *spiritual* suffering in these feelings of abandonment. He was like us in all things, except sin. And he experienced all that we do.

So when you struggle in the spiritual life, when you wonder where God is, when you pray in doubt and darkness, and even when you are close to despair, you are praying to someone who is fully human and fully divine, to someone who understands you fully.

5

Jesus Understands Physical Pain

"I am thirsty."

After this, when Jesus knew that all was now finished, he said (in order to fulfill the scripture), "I am thirsty." A jar full of sour wine was standing there. So they put a sponge full of the wine on a branch of hyssop and held it to his mouth.

J esus had a body.

Let me repeat: Jesus had a body.

Quite a few people have a difficult time accepting Jesus's humanity. Now, I believe, as the church teaches, that Jesus was fully human and fully divine. But some of us focus almost exclusively on stories that seem to highlight his divine nature: the Son of God who went around healing the sick, raising people from the dead, stilling storms—all the kinds of miracles that people tend to associate with his divine power.[1]

In other words, some of us are tempted to believe that God was simply playacting at being human. Just pretending. Some of us say, "Well, he may have suffered on the cross, but for the rest of his life he was God, so he must have had it easier than the rest of us, right?" Or we say, "Well, *technically* he was human, but he was God, so he really didn't have the same experiences I do, right?"

Let's be clear again: Jesus was born, he lived, and he died. The child called Yeshua—his name in Aramaic—entered the world as helpless as any newborn and just as dependent on his parents. He needed to be nursed, held, fed, burped, and changed. As a boy growing up in the minuscule town of Nazareth—which archaeological research shows us had only two to four hundred people—Jesus would have skinned his knees on the rocky ground, bumped his head on doorways, and pricked his fingers on thorns. He would have gotten cuts and bruises like any child.

Jesus had a body like ours. That means he ate like us, drank like us, and slept like us. He went through puberty. As a human being, he would have experienced the normal sexual longings and urges. We know he was unmarried and celibate, but he would have, as a human being, felt all the normal sexual attractions and desires. Those are far from sinful, after all. He may even have fallen in love with a girl in Nazareth.

Jesus had a body. We know that Jesus got tired from time to time. In one Gospel passage he falls asleep in a boat on the Sea of Galilee.[2] Jesus pulled muscles, got headaches, felt sick to his stomach, came down with the flu, and maybe even sprained an ankle or two.

A few years ago, a vicious stomach bug swept through our community. (When you live in a religious community and one person gets sick, it's just a matter of time before everyone else does too.) And one night it hit me: I was the sickest I've ever been. In any event and without going into unnecessary details, when I was hunched with my face over the toilet for the fifth time that night, I had a strange thought: "Jesus did this." Yes, Jesus, indelicate as it may sound, threw up. He was a human being. In fact, he may have had even more severe physical problems than you or I do, since health and sanitation conditions were wretched in first-century Nazareth. (Sewage, for example, would have been simply tossed into alleyways.)

Like all of us, Jesus sweated and sneezed and scratched. Everything proper to the human being, to the human body, he experienced—except sin. These bodily experiences include hunger and, here on the cross, thirst.

Crucifixion was one of the most agonizing ways to die. The Romans devised it precisely because it was. A person was nailed to the cross, usually through the wrists, and then set on a sort of small wooden seat fixed midway on the upright beam. Alternately, a small footrest was placed under the feet. That wasn't for comfort. Rather, it was to prolong the agony. Victims of crucifixion died from either loss of blood or, more likely, asphyxiation, as the weight of the body compressed their rib cage and lungs. With this painful ability to support themselves, as-phyxiation took longer.

In the blazing hot sun of Judea, Jesus would have thirsted.

As an aside, a few years ago on a pilgrimage to the Holy Land, I spent an hour hiking with a friend through a ravine in the Judean Desert, in what I later discovered was the original "Valley of the Shadow of Death." And let me tell you something about the Judean Desert: it's almost unbearably hot. It must have been about 115 degrees. I was the hottest I've ever been in my entire life, and that includes two years working in East Africa.

In the blazing hot sun of Judea, Jesus would have thirsted, because he had a body.

What does Jesus's having a human body mean for each of us? Let me suggest two things. First, something about our world, our community, and our brothers and sisters. Second, something about us as individuals. And the two are connected.

First, a word about our brothers and sisters. Think of the thirstiest you've ever been. Maybe you were running a race on a humid summer morning, or you were walking on the street one blisteringly hot afternoon, or you were in the hospital one night and the nurse forgot to bring you ice chips. Remember how *good* that first drink of water felt. You felt that you couldn't go a moment longer, and when that liquid finally coursed down your throat, it was so glorious, so satisfying, such a relief.

For many people in the world physical thirst is a daily experience. Clean water is not the lot of everyone. All most of us have to do is turn on the tap to slake our thirst, but you might be surprised to learn that nearly eight hundred million people today lack access to clean, fresh water. And it is women and children who are often most affected by these situations, since the burden of procuring water usually falls to them—in bodily form; often they must walk miles to acquire it and carry the heavy liquid back home. It also affects them in terms of lost opportunities for education and earning a living. Finally, many women are physically or sexually assaulted while out getting water.[3]

Since we know that the Body of Christ is all of us, all of our brothers and sisters, you can say that Jesus's Body is going thirsty right now, and is suffering. So if you are sad about Jesus's body having thirsted on the cross two thousand years ago, and even shed a tear, then shed a tear for the members of his Body who are thirsting right now. Shed a tear for those who suffer bodily today—through thirst or hunger or nakedness or imprisonment or torture or famine or assault or abuse.

Shed a tear and try to do something about it. Why not let that sorrow spur you to action? After all, this is one way that God moves us to act.

The second point about Jesus having a body has to do with us as individuals. And it is this: Jesus understands what you are going through physically.

Everyone reading this book has some physical burden that represents a cross in their lives. Perhaps it's something very small, like a cold. Perhaps it's something bigger, like a chronic illness that saps your energy. Perhaps it's something even bigger than that, like struggling with a life-threatening disease. Particularly when the cross is a big one, God can feel far away. And we wonder, "Does God even care?"

But remember this: God had a body. In fact, God *has* a body, because Christ is risen, really and truly. The Risen Christ carries within himself the experiences of his humanity, and that includes suffering. Remember that in one of his first appearances after the Resurrection he showed the disciples his wounds.[4]

That important theological insight often goes overlooked. The Risen Christ is the same person as the Jesus of Nazareth who walked the earth. The Resurrection does not mean that a new person was created after Jesus died. No, it is the same person, and he bears the marks of his physical suffering on his resurrected body. As Jesus says to the apostle Thomas after the Resurrection, "Put your finger here and see my hands. Reach out your hand and put it in my side. Do not doubt but believe."[5]

Stanley Marrow, SJ, a New Testament scholar, summarizes this idea beautifully in his commentary on the Gospel of John:

The risen Lord had to be recognizably and identifiably Jesus of Nazareth, the man whom the disciples knew and followed, whom they saw and heard, with whom they ate and because of whom they now cowered behind closed doors for "fear of the [Jewish leaders]." For him to have risen as any other than the Jesus of Nazareth they knew would void the resurrection of all its meaning. The one they had confessed as their risen Lord is the same Jesus of Nazareth they had known and followed. Showing them "his hands and his side," which bore the marks of the crucifixion and the pierce by the lance, was not a theatrical gesture, but the necessary credentials of the identity of the risen Lord, who stood before them, with the crucified Jesus of Nazareth whom they knew.[6]

Therefore, the Risen Christ *remembers* his suffering.

So when you pray, you are praying not simply to someone who understands you because he is all knowing, all loving, and all compassionate. You're also praying to someone who understands you because *he went through* what you are going through.

And God *wants* you to pray to him. God desires a relationship with you. So much so that God came down to earth and suffered physically for you. That's one reason God comes to us—to help us to be in relationship with him. God wants that so much.

God, you could say, thirsts for it.

6

Jesus Understands Disappointment

"It is finished."

When Jesus had received the wine, he said, "It is finished." Then he bowed his head and gave up his spirit.

Jesus underwent many kinds of sufferings on Good Friday. In general, Christians tend to focus on his physical sufferings. And it is obviously true that he suffered a great deal physically. As I mentioned, crucifixion was one of the most painful deaths imaginable, perfected—if you could use that word—by the Romans for that purpose. The writers of the Gospels, however, are spare in describing it. Matthew, Mark, Luke, and John say almost nothing about the actual act.

It is as if the evangelists could barely bring themselves to describe anything but the naked facts. This is sometimes baffling to those who have seen films or read books, helpful as they are, that focus on the horrible act itself. But there might be another reason for the unadorned descriptions: residents of first-century Palestine, including the early Christians, knew well what crucifixion was. Josephus, the Jewish historian writing around the time of Jesus, reports that after the death of Herod the Great, one Roman general, to quell the ensuing unrest, lined the roads of Galilee with two thousand crosses.[1] People knew what crucifixion was and how victims were crucified.

Victims were first affixed to the kind of the crossbeam that Jesus carried, by ropes or by nails driven through the wrists or forearms. In earlier times that part of the cross was sometimes a simple piece of wood used to bar a door. The crossbeam was set into a vertical wooden beam that stood perhaps six feet high.

To breathe, victims were forced to prop themselves up momentarily on a footrest in order to draw air into their lungs, but the pain in their nailed feet and cramped legs would have gradually made it impossible to support themselves. So they would have slumped down violently, pulling on the nails in their wrists, tearing the skin and ripping the tendons, causing searing pain. The awful process would have been repeated over and over, each time they attempted to breathe. And it would have been almost impossible for any human being (as Jesus was) whose body was involuntarily trying to avoid physical pain not to experience some form of panic. As I have said, victims died from either loss of blood or asphyxiation. There was little need to explain this to the first readers of the Gospels.

The Gospel of Mark simply says, "And they crucified him."[2]

Jesus may have been stripped of his garments and left naked, completing the shaming intention of crucifixion. But we do not know this for certain. The Roman practice was to crucify the victim naked, but New Testament scholars say that as a nod to Jewish sensibilities he might have worn a loincloth, as seen in popular depictions. But that's the most he would have been wearing.

Pontius Pilate's inscription—"Jesus of Nazareth, the King of the Jews"—which Mark's Gospel calls the "accusation" or "charge," was affixed to the wooden cross as a warning to insurrectionists or anyone with messianic designs. Beside Jesus were crucified two thieves, though the Greek word used may also imply a kind of Robin Hood figure—"social bandits," as some scholars suggest.[3] But no matter what kind of thieves these two men were, Jesus died as he lived—in solidarity with outcasts, in this case criminals.

It was a public spectacle calculated not only to warn but also to magnify the shame for the victim, who suffered an agonizing death. All were invited to watch and comment. The Gospel of Mark describes passersby openly scorning him.[4]

Most of us, then, are aware of the physical pain that Jesus underwent, which is the theme of a great deal of Christian art, with a focus on Jesus's face contorted in pain and the mutilated body writhing in agony. We have already described the emotional pain of abandonment by his friends and the spiritual pain of feeling aban-doned by God. So we cannot underestimate the combined physical, emotional, and spiritual pain that Jesus experienced.

But there is another suffering that we may overlook: the suffering of wondering whether his "work" would continue after his death. Here we enter into some speculation about what Jesus was feeling on the cross. Of course the Seven Last Words offer us a privileged window into his feelings, but not a complete one. Questions remain. And although we are not told explic-itly by the Gospels, it's important to meditate on such questions, for they invite us into a deeper understanding of Jesus, and therefore a deeper relationship with him.

In his classic text *The Spiritual Exercises,* for ex-ample, St. Ignatius invites us, as a way of praying, to picture ourselves at all the important moments of Jesus's life, including the Crucifixion, and ask ourselves: What was it like for him?

Did Jesus, for example, know what was going to happen after the Crucifixion?

You could argue that he did, because he said, "Destroy this temple, and in three days I will raise it up."[5] By the same token, there are signs that he didn't know, for example, when he agonizes in the garden. And even if he understood *something* about his rising from the dead, there is the possibility that, as he hung on the cross, he still may have wondered whether what he had done would endure, whether the apostles understood what he had asked of them, whether the disciples heard what he had to say, and whether his followers would be able to continue with what he charged them to do. In other words, whether part of what you might call his "project" would survive.

That is a kind of suffering too, the suffering of seeing something seemingly come to an end. The suffering of knowing that something may be over. Perhaps this can be seen as another way to think about the words "It is finished."

Now, to be clear, almost all New Testament scholars say that in John's Gospel the words "It is finished" refer to the fulfillment of the

Father's will and of Jesus's mission, as in, "It is completed."[6] In other words, "I have done the task that the Father has asked me to do." Indeed, in the overall theology of the Gospel of John, Jesus's total self-offering on the cross is the paradigm par excellence of God's love. Earlier in the Gospel, for example, John says that Jesus loved his friends "to the end," in other words, to the end of his life, or as completely as he could.[7]

Stanley Marrow reminds us of this in his commentary on the Gospel of John. After eating a Passover meal, Jesus, about to be crucified, says, "Now the Son of Man has been glorified, and God has been glorified in him."[8] Father Marrow writes: "In his death on the cross, Jesus reveals who he really is: the revealer of the Father." Why? Because at that moment, Jesus shows us the depth of his love for us. "Thus, in his death on the cross, in the totality of his obedience to the will of the one who sent him, he reveals his privileged identity as the only Son."[9]

So there is a kind of "completion" or, to use Jesus's words, a "finish." This is most likely what those words mean, at least as John is presenting them.

But let's look at this in another, more speculative, way. Many of us who read those words may also hear in them a kind of resignation that echoes our own experiences, as in, "I have done all that I can do. I cannot do any more."

Some of us may even hear in Jesus's words a sense of disappointment. As I said, we are now entering into speculative territory, but I think it's worth thinking about the possibility that Jesus may have felt a sense of concern or even disappointment about what would happen after his death.

Think about the days, months, and years that Jesus poured into his ministry. First, think of his decades-long preparation, as he prayed about his vocation as a young man, decided to seek out baptism from John, and then underwent his grueling testing in the desert. Think of the effort that went into choosing the apostles and patiently teaching them, as well as the incredible energy expended in traveling, healing, and preaching to people throughout Judea, Galilee, and beyond—all work undertaken to help people understand what it meant to be invited into the reign of God.

Now think of Jesus on the cross, knowing not only that he had done all he could for the Father, but perhaps wondering what would happen to his circle of followers after his death and whether his "project" would continue.

What do I mean by this? That Jesus had failed? By no means. Indeed, his mission was to reveal and make present the reign of God, which he had accomplished. Rather, he may have wondered if his disciples would continue after his death. Accepting the possibility that his "project" might not endure must have been difficult.

After all, Jesus had seen how his disciples repeatedly responded to his message not with understanding, but with confusion. He had seen them fail to grasp the meaning of his parables and teachings and even misunderstand the significance of his miracles. Remember, he says to those around him, "You faithless and perverse generation, how much longer must I be with you? How much longer must I put up with you?"[10] He knew that the twelve apostles sometimes responded not with faith but with doubt, not with humility but with pride. In fact, immediately after he predicts his own suffering, James and John, the sons of Zebedee, start to argue about who was going to be first in the reign of God.[11] Jesus knew that they often responded not with courage but fear; after all, he had just watched them scatter in the garden.

So, as he hung on the cross, what might he have thought?

As I said, we are entering into speculative territory, but it's helpful for us to ask: What might have been going through the mind of the man who said he felt abandoned by God? Did he wonder if these men—who had misunderstood him, jockeyed for position, and abandoned him—would know what to do? Did he think his mission of preaching the good news would continue with them? And although the Gospel of Matthew tells us that he had appointed

Peter as head of his church, what did Jesus think about the future of that church as he hung on the cross?[12] Remember that Peter denied even *knowing* him just a few hours ago and had also just abandoned him.

So although Jesus may have said, "It is finished," referring to the completion of his task, he may also have thought, "It is over," when he thought of what would happen after his death. In this situation, again, Jesus may understand us very well.

All of us have seen things come to a sad end, seen a project fail. You poured your heart and soul into something you planned for, saved for, hoped for. You had such high hopes and now, apparently, it has come to naught. It's a terrible feeling.

Maybe you didn't get into the college you wanted. Maybe you had hopes for a career that never materialized. Maybe you lost your house in a fire or a hurricane. Maybe your dreams for a lasting marriage have been dashed. Maybe your desire to get married at all was never fulfilled.

Maybe your dreams for your children, or even to have children, never came true. Maybe you've lost the health you once had.

So one day you say to yourself, with infinite sadness, "It's over," or, "It is finished."

Jesus is with you on this. We cannot be sure, but it's reasonable to think that as he hung on the cross—abandoned, bereft, and in pain—he may have wondered what was going to happen to his disciples after his death. Would they continue to strive to live as he did? Would they put into practice his words? Would they believe in the miracles they had witnessed? Would they love one another? Almost as difficult as the physical and spiritual pain is the pain of lost possibilities.

Yet in all of this we have Easter Sunday. Good Friday makes no sense without Easter Sunday. Jesus may have felt that the disciples would never gather again or even that his teachings would be forgotten, but the Father had other plans.

As he hung on the cross, readying to die, readying to turn himself completely over to the Father, Jesus may not have been able to see how his work would continue. But the Father did, for God can use everything we bring to him and magnify it—even our dashed hopes. And just as Jesus multiplied the loaves and fishes for the crowds during his public ministry, God can take what we offer and multiply it.

We may feel that our dreams are ending, but God has other dreams for us.

We may feel that things have not worked out, but God has other workings in mind.

We may feel that hope is dead, but God is the source of all hope.

"All shall be well, all shall be well, and all manner of thing shall be well," as Blessed Julian of Norwich, the fourteenth-century English mystic, once wrote.[13]

Or as the contemporary saying goes, all will be well in the end. And if all is not well, then it is not the end.

Jesus Understands Self-Offering

*"Father, into your hands
I commend my spirit."*

It was now about noon, and darkness came over the whole land until three in the afternoon, while the sun's light failed; and the curtain of the temple was torn in two. Then Jesus, crying with a loud voice, said, "Father, into your hands I commend my spirit." Having said this, he breathed his last. When the centurion saw what had taken place, he praised God and said, "Certainly this man was innocent." And when all the crowds who had gathered there for this spectacle saw what had taken place, they returned home, beating their breasts. But all his acquaintances, including the women who had followed him from Galilee, stood at a distance, watching these things.

D id Jesus know what would happen on Easter Sunday? As we close our meditations, I would like to invite you to return to that important question.

The New Testament is of two minds on this. On the one hand, Jesus says clearly, "Destroy this temple, and in three days I will raise it up."[1] He predicts his Resurrection several times in the Gospels. On the other hand, Jesus clearly agonizes in the garden and feels abandoned on the cross, both of which make less sense if he knew what awaited him on Easter Sunday.

Here we enter even more deeply into the mystery of Jesus's identity. As a fully divine person, Jesus would have known all things, with the consciousness of God the Father. Therefore, he would have fully anticipated the Resurrection. But as a fully human person he would have known only what a human being could know, for to be fully human means having a human mind, a human consciousness, a human way of knowing. By that logic, he could not have known what would happen to him after the Crucifixion.

More to the point, who did Jesus think he was? Did he understand himself as the Messiah? The Gospels show demons declaring him the Messiah several times: "I know who you are, the Holy One of God," shouts the "man with an unclean spirit" in the synagogue at Capernaum, upon seeing Jesus.[2] The demon knows. St. Peter does as well, as when he says, "You are the Messiah, the Son of the living God."[3] And Jesus accepts this proclamation. Still, divinity was not part of the Jewish concept of the Messiah at that time.

So how did he come to understand himself? His identity? His humanity? His divinity?

Much of this must remain a mystery. But one helpful way to understand it is that Jesus grew in his understanding of his identity throughout his life.

To begin with, it is reasonable to think that Mary would have shared with her son her experience with the Angel Gabriel, and Joseph his experiences of his dreams. All parents want to help their children understand who they are called to be, so why wouldn't Mary and Joseph try to help Jesus understand his unique vocation? As he matured, they likely spoke with him about his identity, even if they didn't fully comprehend it themselves. Much later, of course, at his baptism, Jesus has a profound experience of himself as God's "beloved son."[4]

But even after his baptism, Jesus may have struggled to understand what this meant. We all do the same after we have had a deep insight or passed a milestone in our lives. A married couple, for example, don't fully understand marriage on their wedding day. A mother doesn't fully understand motherhood on the day of the birth of her first child. And a priest doesn't fully understand what it means to be a priest on the day of his ordination. All of this takes time. So perhaps it took time for Jesus to understand what it meant to be God's "beloved son." After all, what is traditionally considered Jesus's first miracle seems to be a reluctant one. At the Wedding Feast at Cana, Mary has to encourage him to do the miracle. But after her prompting, he does it.[5]

After that the miracles flow out of him like water. He heals a man possessed by a demon in the synagogue. He cures a paralyzed man carried to him by friends. He stills a storm on the Sea of Galilee. He multiplies the loaves and the fishes. He restores sight to the blind. He makes the lame walk. He raises people from the dead. As he performed these miracles, his identity undoubtedly became clearer to him. Now I may be wrong and Jesus may have known precisely who he was from the first moment of his consciousness, but it is also reasonable to suggest that Jesus gradually *grew* in the knowledge of who he was: the Son of God.

All along, though, there was one thing Jesus knew for sure: his governing desire was to do his Father's will. Here is another intersection between Jesus's life and ours.

At every step of the way, even if he may not have fully understood his vocation, Jesus is trying to carry out the Father's will. And in the garden of Gethsemane he reaches the ultimate decision point. Gethsemane is one of the clearest windows into his humanity, for Jesus doesn't immediately say, "Oh, yes, God, whatever you want."

No, first he says, "Remove this cup from me." Only then does he say, "Yet, not what I want, but what you want."[6] This is an utterly human response to impending suffering. And perhaps even Jesus didn't know what was going to happen after he made this final offering on the cross.

When I celebrate Mass I'm almost always moved by the words, "Take this, all of you, and eat of it. This is my body." Catholics believe that Jesus gives us his body in this way in the Eucharist.

But Jesus gave of his body in another way as well during his time on earth. He *took* his body throughout the land then called Palestine, walking from town to town, giving himself to people, listening to them, healing them, feeding them, doing whatever the Father asked of him. He gave of himself in his public ministry. And on the cross he gives himself over completely: "Into your hands I commend my spirit."

It is the greatest sacrifice the world has ever seen: body and soul he gives himself. Jesus gives himself entirely.

This is what we're all called to do: give ourselves totally to God.

What does it mean to give ourselves entirely to God? At the most basic level, it means following God's commandments and living a Christian life. But it also means something else. Let me suggest two things.

First, it means holding nothing back from God. There's often a part of our lives that we keep from God: a grudge, a sinful habit, a pattern of selfish behavior, a desire for status and power, a need to acquire more possessions. In general, we lead good lives, but we usually withhold a part of ourselves from God. We say, "You can have everything else, God, but not this." But we are asked to turn it *all* over to God.

Second, giving ourselves entirely to God means surrendering to the future God has in store for us. We may not know what it is. We may not understand it. We may even fear it. But we are called to surrender ourselves to that future. As Jesus did.

What will happen when we surrender? We can't know.

Did Jesus know? For me, Jesus's sacrifice on Good Friday is even more powerful if he did not fully know what awaited him. Maybe on Easter Sunday even Jesus Christ was surprised. Perhaps he fully knew only *then* who he was. As one theologian has written, on Easter Sunday perhaps Jesus's identity "burst upon him in all clarity."[7] On Easter he knew—fully. Soon the disciples would know too. Soon the whole world would know.

Here is yet another intersection with our lives, another place where Jesus understands us. Jesus understands that when we give ourselves to the Father, we may not know what kind of new life will come from our offering. And he knows that the more we give ourselves to the Father, the more new life can come from whatever we give.

The more we give of ourselves, the more we know who we are.

The more we give of ourselves, the fuller lives we will lead.

And so, into your hands, O God, we commend our spirits.

The Understanding Christ

Good Friday was a single day in Jesus's life. In other words, Jesus's life was not *all* suffering and pain. As I mentioned, most of his public ministry was centered on joy. Indeed, when Jesus encountered suffering of any kind, his first response, after listening to the person's problems, was to alleviate the suffering.

Think of the man who, paralyzed for thirty-eight years, sat by the Pool of Bethesda in Jerusalem, hoping for a cure.[1] The pool's waters were supposed to have healing powers, thought to be strongest when the water was stirred up. At the time, it was believed that an angel stirred up the waters; in reality, the movement of the underground currents feeding the pool caused disturbances on the surface.[2]

When Jesus encounters the paralyzed man, he listens patiently. "Sir," the man says to Jesus, "I have no one to put me into the pool when the water is stirred up; and while I am making my way, someone else steps down ahead of me." Jesus lets him share his story and then heals him, saying, "Stand up, take your mat and walk." For those who were suffering at the time, an encounter with Jesus meant the *end* of suffering. So it is misleading to focus on Jesus's life as a kind of glorification of suffering or sadness.

Moreover, imagine what it must have been like to see Jesus bringing an end to suffering, as when he effected one of his miraculous healings. The Gospels most often talk about "amazement" or "astonishment" among the disciples and onlookers, but for those afflicted, and for their friends and family, there must have been exceeding, almost uncontainable, joy. Imagine the reaction, for example, of Jairus, a synagogue official whose daughter is thought to be dead, until Jesus enters his house and brings the little girl back to life.[3] Joy! Imagine the response of the "Widow of Nain," whose dead son is about to be buried, until Jesus restores him to life in her presence.[4] Joy! How could this father and mother feel anything *other* than joy? And after the Resurrection, the words "joy" and "rejoice" are used time and again by the Gospel writers: "The disciples rejoiced when they saw the Lord,"[5] says John. Jesus's Resurrection, and his earlier deeds, brought joy.

So did his words. Jesus's preaching was meant to bring joy to those who followed him. His words were, after all, good news. "Rejoice and be glad," he says at the conclusion of the Sermon on the Mount.[6] Indeed, of his purpose he says, "I have said these things to you so that my joy may be in you, and that your joy may be complete."[7]

Jesus's public ministry was largely a ministry of joy, not suffering. Encountering him meant encountering the joy that characterizes the reign of God. So we should not reduce his life simply to that of the "Suffering Servant," as important as that image is in the Gospels (particularly in Mark), or of the traditional "Man of Sorrows."

Still, Jesus suffered. Even before he stepped onto the world stage, during his life in Nazareth Jesus suffered the physical and emotional aches and pains of a human life, including seeing Joseph (and certainly other relatives) fall ill and die. During his public ministry, he suffered as well. When he began preaching in his hometown, the townspeople were so offended by what he said (he declared himself the fulfillment of Scripture) that they tried to throw him off a cliff.[8] At one point, as we have seen, his mother and extended family went to Capernaum to collect him, since they apparently thought he was "out of his mind."[9] The disciples didn't always understand him. In fact, they occasionally did the opposite of what he wanted them to do—for example, arguing about who would be seated next to Jesus in heaven.[10] He was persecuted frequently by some religious authorities. He wept at the death of his friend Lazarus.[11] Thus, the sufferings of human life were not unknown to him.

And as we have seen, on Good Friday he clearly felt abandoned by his friends and by the Father, experienced physical pain, and suffered disappointment. And given that all of his last words are probably not recorded in the Gospels, he may have suffered other things—emotional pain and struggle—that we can only guess at.

What does this mean for us? How does Jesus's suffering change us? Help us? What does it mean to have an understanding Christ? Let me suggest a few things.

First, it helps us to feel less alone. There are few things as isolating as suffering, for everyone's suffering is largely incommunicable. The particular problems that you face in your family, for example, are so complex, so shot through with complicated family histories and relationships, as to be almost unexplainable to others. Struggles in your workplace are also complex, hard to explain. The physical problems you deal with are by their very nature private, since no one else can climb into your body and experience your pain. Overall, the struggles you face about almost any part of your life are so private, so personal, and so unique, that even when you do explain them, you may feel that you've given someone the wrong impression.

But there is one person who understands you fully: the Risen Christ.

Jesus understands your human life because he *lived* a human life. So you are never alone in your suffering. The Risen Christ—alive and present to us in the Holy Spirit—is with you in your suffering. He is with you in his *divinity*—that is, he knows all things and therefore understands your suffering fully. And he is with you in his *humanity*—he experienced all of these things. If you've ever felt alone in your struggles, you no longer have to. You can know that Jesus understands you in every way. And when you pray to Jesus, you are praying to someone who understands you. This may help you to feel less alone.

Second, knowing that Jesus understands you may help you speak to Jesus more openly in prayer. Perhaps you've had the following experience. You are facing a difficult problem and struggle to talk about it. It's hard to find the words, you're not certain that people will understand, and you're worried that people might think you're just complaining. Suddenly you meet someone who is going through the same thing. Perhaps you've met someone who lost a parent, just as you have. Perhaps you've met a person who is looking for work, as you are. Perhaps you've even found a support group of people living with the same illness you have. Suddenly you feel more at ease and can open up. It's a relief to be able to let down your guard and speak candidly with that person or group.

You can do the same with Jesus. Let your guard down. Open up. Be honest with him in prayer. It's a relief to be honest after feeling that you won't be understood, that you can't complain, that you can't ask for help, that you can't even mention your struggles. No, Jesus wants to hear about your struggles, and he understands them.

Third, knowing about Jesus's suffering helps you to understand Jesus himself. For many people God seems utterly unknowable. In part, this is true. God is essentially unable to be fully comprehended, known, or defined by us. As the saying goes, if you can know it, understand it, or define it, then "it" is not God.

Yet God can be known through Jesus. One reason that God became human is so that we could begin to understand God. God comes to us in the most familiar and accessible way possible—as one of us—to help us enter into a deeper relationship with God.

For many people, though, even Jesus can be hard to come to know. When we imagine him performing his great miracles—healing the sick, stilling storms, raising people from the dead— it's hard to think that our initial reaction to him would be anything other than the same kind of "amazement" the disciples experienced. Or perhaps fear—the kind of fear that the disciples felt when they saw him calm a storm.

Not long ago, for example, I was on a pilgrimage with fifty others to the Holy Land. Included in the pilgrimage was a boat ride on the Sea of Galilee. Now, when a boat ride was proposed to us by our travel agency, I rolled my eyes. It sounded unbearably cheesy.

Stepping aboard the motor-powered wooden boat didn't allay my fears of cheesiness. Our tour guide quietly relayed the offers of the boat's captain. Did we want him to play the "Star-Spangled Banner" as we left the harbor? We did not. Did we want him to play gospel music as we plowed out to sea? We did not. Did we want him to cast a net off the boat as if he were a fisherman? We did not.

Instead, we asked the captain to simply turn

off the engines while a Jesuit priest read aloud the Gospel passage that tells of Jesus stilling the storm. After the engine was silenced, it was just us and the sea.

And the wind. The plastic pennants that hung from a thin rope strung around the boat snapped loudly in the strong wind. Then I imagined what it would be like if the wind stopped suddenly—at someone's word. I realized how terrified the disciples must have been, and a wave of pity for them swept over me. "Who then is this," they said, "that even the wind and the sea obey him?"[12] How could the disciples have been anything *but* afraid? It's incredible that after *any* of the miracles they could have been with Jesus without fear.

One line in the Greek has always stayed with me: "They feared a great fear," says the Gospel of Mark after Jesus stills the storm.[13] When we imagine the miracles and think of Jesus, we can grow fearful. Likewise, seeing Jesus perform miracles would make many of us simply want to worship him.

Consequently, it can be hard for some people to feel that they can know Jesus. But there are many windows into his human life. One is remembering that he lived a fully human life as a boy, an adolescent, and young adult in Nazareth. Another is recalling that he spent eighteen years of his life working—earning his "daily bread," as many of us do. Another is thinking about his friendships with the disciples and people like Mary, Martha, and their brother Lazarus. The Gospel of John points out in no uncertain terms: "Jesus loved Martha and her sister and Lazarus."[14] Each of these human experiences offers us a window into Jesus's life.

Good Friday is another important entrée into his life. Through his Seven Last Words we are invited to come to know him more deeply. Imagine a friend asking you to accompany him or her through a difficult time—the loss of a job, the death of a parent, major surgery. You would see your friend at his or her most vulnerable, most naked, most honest. It would be a privilege to accompany your friend in that way—it's something that would change your relationship forever.

The Seven Last Words are such an invitation. They offer us a privileged access into Jesus's life and therefore an entrée into who he is. They help to reveal him to us more fully.

Jesus, then, becomes someone whom we can understand better, as we would want to understand any friend. And he becomes someone with whom we can enter more deeply into relationship.

Which is what Jesus thirsts for.

ACKNOWLEDGMENTS

I am very grateful to Timothy Cardinal Dolan, the archbishop of New York, for inviting me to preach the Seven Last Words at the beautiful St. Patrick's Cathedral on Good Friday of 2015. During the long service (nearly three hours) Cardinal Dolan sat in the bishop's seat and listened attentively. At the third Word, however, he stood up and exited the sanctuary. *Well,* I thought, *it's a busy day for him, so it's not surprising that he wouldn't stay for the whole service.*

But I was wrong. A few minutes later he reappeared carrying a bottle of water for me, thinking that I might be thirsty. Then he sat down and listened to the rest of the service. Thus, I'm grateful for his invitation and care overall.

I'm also very grateful to Joseph McAuley, assistant editor at *America,* for helping me input the edits and changes to the manuscript. I'm grateful to Mickey Maudlin and Mark Tauber at HarperOne for their encouragement, to Ann Moru for her careful edits, to Noël Chrisman for her care of the book, and to Adrian Morgan for the lovely cover. I'm also happy that Heidi Hill is such a terrific fact checker; she saved me from a few misquotations of the New Testament.

Most of all, I'm grateful to Jesus for calling me into the Society named for him, and still more for his infinite and understanding love.

NOTES

Introduction: The Seven Last Words

1. Raymond E. Brown's magnificent book on the last days of Jesus, *The Death of the Messiah* (2 vols.; New York: Doubleday, 1994), makes this point in a short overview of the Seven Last Words (2: 971).

2. This process is elaborated in John P. Meier's *A Marginal Jew,* vol. 1 (New York: Doubleday, 1991), pp. 41–48. The idea of the multistage development of the Gospels is supported by all contemporary New Testament scholars.

3. Other ancillary figures, like Simon of Cyrene, who helped to carry Jesus's cross in the Passion, could also have provided eyewitness accounts.

4. "Gospel" is derived from the Old English *godspel,* or "good news." "Evangelist" is from the Greek *euangelion,* "good news" or "good message."

5. Daniel J. Harrington, SJ, *Jesus: A Historical Portrait* (Cincinnati: St. Anthony Messenger, 2007), p. 7. Traditionally, Mark was seen as relying heavily on Peter's testimony, Luke was associated with Paul, and John with the "Beloved Disciple" mentioned in that Gospel.

6. This source is nicknamed "Q" by scholars, after the German *Quelle,* meaning "source."

7. Brown, *Death of the Messiah,* 2: 972.

8. Heb. 4:15.

9. For more on this, see my book *Between Heaven and Mirth: Why Joy, Humor, and Laughter Are at the Heart of the Spiritual Life* (San Francisco: HarperOne, 2011).

10. Matt. 11:18–19; Luke 7:33–34.

Chapter 1: Jesus Understands the Challenge of Forgiveness

1. Jeanne Bishop, "Lord, Have Mercy," *America,* April 6, 2015.

2. "Deliver me from my enemies, O my God; / protect me from those who rise up against me. / Deliver me from those who work evil; / from the bloodthirsty save me" (Ps. 59:1–2).

3. According to Raymond Brown, "This act of forgiveness covered the Romans who physically affixed Jesus to the cross but did not understand that they were doing this outrage to God's Son" (*The Death of the Messiah,* 2 vols. [New York: Doubleday, 1994], 2: 973).

4. Luke 5:1–11.

5. Luke 19:1–10.

6. John 8:1–11.

Chapter 2: Jesus Understands Doubts About the Afterlife

1. Christopher O'Mahony, OCD, ed., *St. Thérèse of Lisieux by Those Who Knew Her* (Dublin: Veritas, 1975), p. 195.

2. John 11:25–26.

3. John 14:2.

4. 1 Cor. 15:20.

5. Lev. 23:9–14.

6. Rom. 8:38–39.

Chapter 3: Jesus Understands a Parent's Love

1. The full prayer, the first half of which is inspired by the Annunciation in the Gospel of Luke, is: "Hail Mary, full of grace. The Lord is with thee. Blessed art thou among women, and blessed is the fruit of thy womb, Jesus. Holy Mary, Mother

of God, pray for us sinners, now and at the hour of our death. Amen."

2. Luke 1:34.

3. Of course it may sound strange to say "Jesus *has* a body," rather than "Jesus *had* a body," but Christian theology holds that at the Ascension, Jesus was taken up body and soul into heaven. So it's good to remember that, in some mysterious way, Jesus still has a body.

4. Mark 3:32.

5. Mark 3:21.

6. Mark 3:33–35.

7. Daniel J. Harrington, SJ, *The Gospel of Matthew,* Sacra Pagina Series (Collegeville, MN: Liturgical, 2007), p. 192.

8. That is, just his "mother and brothers" (and "sisters," depending on the Gospel) travel to Capernaum, but not Joseph.

9. John 2:1–12.

Chapter 4: Jesus Understands Feelings of Abandonment

1. Ps. 22:24.

2. Raymond E. Brown, *The Death of the Messiah,* 2 vols. (New York: Doubleday, 1994), 2: 1043–58.

3. Mark 14:36.

4. Mother Teresa, *Come Be My Light* (New York: Doubleday, 2007), pp. 192–93. In this book of collected letters, Mother Teresa speaks at length about her feelings of abandonment.

Chapter 5: Jesus Understands Physical Pain

1. Remember, Jesus Christ is fully human and fully divine at all times. No matter how much one Gospel passage seems to illustrate one or the other "nature," he is always both. Thus, he is divine when sawing a plank of wood in Nazareth and human when stilling a storm.

2. Mark 4:38; Luke 8:23.

3. Based on an interview with Christiana Peppard, author of *Just Water: Theology, Ethics, and the Global Water Crisis* (Mary-knoll, NY: Orbis Books, 2014).

4. John 20:20.

5. John 20:27.

6. Stanley B. Marrow, SJ, *The Gospel of John: A Reading* (Mahwah, NJ: Paulist, 1995), p. 360.

Chapter 6: Jesus Understands Disappointment

1. Josephus, *The Antiquities of the Jews,* 17.10.10.

2. Mark 15:24.

3. John R. Donahue, SJ, and Daniel J. Harrington, SJ, *The Gospel of Mark,* Sacra Pagina Series (Collegeville, MN: Liturgical, 2002), p. 443.

4. Mark 15:29–32.

5. John 2:19; Mark 14:58; Matt. 26:61.

6. Francis J. Moloney, SDB, *The Gospel of John,* Sacra Pagina Series (Collegeville, MN: Liturgical, 1998). Moloney says that the phrase "is a final cry of triumph, bringing to a conclusion Jesus' earlier promise of the perfection of a task that had been given to him by the Father" (p. 508).

7. This summary is taken from a helpful letter to me from Thomas D. Stegman, SJ, professor of New Testament at Boston College. "By Johannine theology," he writes, "this is the perfection/completion of Jesus's revelation of God's love (cf. John 13:1: He loved his own *eis telos,* that is, to the end of his life and more, by the complete offering of his life in love.)"

8. John 13:31.

9. Stanley B. Marrow, SJ, *The Gospel of John: A Reading* (Mahwah, NJ: Paulist, 1995), p. 241.

10. Matt. 17:17; Luke 9:41.

11. Mark 10:35–45.

12. Matt. 16:18.

13. Julian of Norwich, *Revelations of Divine Love,* chap. 27. Here Julian is quoting from a mystical vision in which Christ spoke to her. So these are, according to Julian, Jesus's words to her.

Chapter 7: Jesus Understands Self-Offering

1. John 2:19.

2. Mark 1:24. Also, see Matt. 8:29: "What have you to do with us, Son of God?" say the "legion" of demons that possess the Gerasene demoniac.

3. Matt. 16:16; Mark 8:29.

4. Matt. 3:13–17; Mark 1:9–11; Luke 3:21–22; John 1:29–34.

5. John 2:1–11.

6. Mark 14:32–36; Matt. 26:36–39; Luke 22:39–42.

7. Elizabeth A. Johnson, *Consider Jesus: Waves of Renewal in Christology* (New York: Crossroad, 1991), p. 42.

Conclusion: The Understanding Christ

1. John 5:1–18.

2. You can see the Pool of Bethesda in Jerusalem today, still fed by those underground currents.

3. Matt 9:18–26; Mark 5:21–43; Luke 8:40–56.

4. Luke 7:11–17.

5. John 20:20.

6. Matt. 5:1–12.

7. John 15:11.

8. Luke 4:16–30; Matt. 13:54–58; Mark 6:1–6.

9. Mark 3:21: "When his family heard it, they went out to restrain him, for people were saying, 'He has gone out of his mind.'"

10. Mark 10:37.

11. John 11:35.

12. Mark 4:35–41; Matt. 8:18, 23–27; Luke 8:22–25; John 6:16–21.

13. Mark 4:41. The Greek is *Ephobēthēsan phobon megan:* literally, "They feared a great fear."

14. John 11:5.